Waltham Forest Libraries

Please return this item by the last date stamped. The loan may be renewed unless required by another customer.

May 2018		
22/09/18		

Need to renew your books?
http://www.walthamforest.gov.uk/libraries or
Dial 0333 370 4700 for Callpoint – our 24/7 automated telephone renewal line. You will need your library card number and your PIN. If you do not know your PIN, contact your local library.

Banthology

Stories From Unwanted Nations

Edited by Sarah Cleave

First published in Great Britain in 2018 by Comma Press.
www.commapress.co.uk

Co-published in the United States by Deep Vellum Press.

A CIP catalogue record of this book is available from the British Library.

ISBN-10 1910974366
ISBN-13 9781910974360

The publisher gratefully acknowledges the support of Arts Council England.

Supported using public funding by
**ARTS COUNCIL
ENGLAND**

Printed and bound in England by Clays Ltd.

Contents

Introduction

Give me your tired, your poor,
Your huddled masses yearning to breathe free,
The wretched refuse of your teeming shore.
Send these, the homeless, tempest-tost to me,
I lift my lamp beside the golden door!
                                        – *Emma Lazarus*

IN JANUARY 2017, PRESIDENT Trump signed Executive Order 13769, banning people from seven Muslim-majority countries – Iran, Iraq, Syria, Yemen, Somalia, Sudan and Libya – from entering the United States for 90 days. It also halted refugee resettlement for 120 days and banned Syrian refugees indefinitely. Although nationality-based travel bans were nothing new – the 1882 Chinese Exclusion Act stayed on the statute book until 1943 – this was the first such piece of legislation in the modern era, and the first that appeared to discriminate along religious lines. The order has since been blocked, challenged, revised, and added to, but the purpose and effect of the ban are obvious, evolving from Trump's presidential campaign pledge to perform a 'total and complete shutdown' of Muslims entering the US. The enforcement of the order – dubbed the 'Muslim ban' by those rallying against it – has been both inhumane and unconstitutional, disrupting tens of thousands of lives and tearing families apart.

The idea for this book was born amid the chaos of that first ban, and sought to champion, give voice to, and better understand a set of nations that the White House would like us to believe are populated entirely by terrorists. As publishers, we are acutely aware of the importance of cultural exchange between communities, and have also seen first-hand the damage caused by tightened visa controls and existing travel restrictions, not just on artists, but on their families – that is to say the damage that impacts on all citizens of nations targeted by prejudicial border controls.

Good stories help us to make sense of the world. They invite us to discover what it's like to be someone else, someone arbitrarily defined as 'other' by the new context they find themselves in; they can also help us to explore the uglier moments of history; times of conflict, oppression or censorship. The writers gathered in this collection were asked to develop a fictional response to Trump's discriminatory ban, exploring themes of exile, travel and restrictions on movement. In doing so, we hoped to provide a space for writers to unpick some of the troubles of the present, and to provide alternative narratives and perspectives. That said, we were concerned not to limit the type of stories that writers from these nations were able to tell. After 9/11, there was an increased interest in writing and culture from the Middle East and North Africa, but a great deal of the narratives commissioned and promoted by publishers had a tendency to essentialise Arab subjects, meaning that the writers themselves had to bear the burden of representing an entire region or country.

The stories collected here have been written by authors from various generations, and offer up a variety of styles. We wanted to showcase as many different experiences as possible, as the travel ban not only affects those living inside the so-called 'banned nations', but also those that have sought peace and freedom in exile. One of the authors, Anoud, moved to New York from Iraq just a month before the first travel ban came in to place, and was, like many others, scared to leave in case she wasn't allowed to return. Her story is a portrait of a young Iraqi woman separated from her family and haunted by the horrors of her past, from the Bush Administration's 'War on Terror' to Trump's so-called Muslim ban. Other stories in the collection explore the perils of the immigration system and the personal and emotional impact of restrictions of movement. Ubah Cristina Ali Farah's story is an evocative, supernatural tale about a young woman's journey from war-torn Somalia, and her hopes of being reunited with her mother and sister. Fereshteh Molavi's story 'Phantom Limb' explores themes of loss, as well as creative expression, following four refugees trying to make a new life for themselves in North America.

Many of the characters in this collection undertake arduous, and sometimes absurd journeys, like the narrator of Najwa Binshatwan's story who is stripped, searched and threatened with eternal hellfire while airport-hopping across the planet to reach her husband. Similarly, Zaher Omareen's protagonist in 'The Beginners Guide to Smuggling' must overcome overweight co-passengers, fake passports and snarling dogs in this darkly comic account of one man's journey from Syria to Sweden via France. Some travellers aren't quite so lucky, never reaching their destination or fulfilling their promise. Rania Mamoun's young protagonist dreams of being born in the form of a bird so that she can escape her life and begin again, far away from her overbearing brother. The final story in this collection, 'The Slow Man' by Wajdi al-Ahdal reimagines the story of Yusuf (also known as Joseph), offering us a stark reminder that we live in an interconnected world in which our actions shape the future.

In some small way, these stories demonstrate the value and responsibility of literature during times of upheaval. Reading can be an escape, something transportative that takes you to different countries, cultures and states of mind.

INTRODUCTION

It can take you to all the places that Donald Trump doesn't want you to go.

Sarah Cleave
Comma Press, Manchester, December 2017

Bird of Paradise

Rania Mamoun

Translated from the Arabic by Ruth Ahmedzai Kemp

THE LITTLE GIRL'S LAUGHTER jars on my ears. I turn to look at her. She dashes through the airport lounge, brandishing her doll with a buoyancy unsuited to the time of day. As she gets closer the girl slows down almost to a stop, glowering at me as if I'd somehow disturbed her precious world order. I give her an apologetic smile and wave. She raises her hand nonchalantly as if to say, 'Don't worry – you're not in the way.'

It is 3am now and the lounge is almost empty. The occasional traveller shuffles through quietly with lowered eyes. The lounge, like the rest of the airport, is a transitory place. But for me, it has become more than that. I've been here for over a week now, glued to this seat which I also use as a bed. The good thing about airports is the freedom to sit wherever you like; no one asks you to leave or to move on. I sit here day in, day out, utterly bereft of everything. The few coins I brought with me are already spent and my pockets are now empty. I ate my last biscuit two days ago; half in the morning, half in the evening. All that remains is regret.

I go to the bathroom which welcomes me once or twice a day. I drink from the tap whenever I feel the pinch of hunger. I can probably survive on water for another week or so, then I'll have to take desperate measures. Last week, I saw a woman grab an entire chicken from the grill at one of the restaurants

1

and run as fast as she could, chased by the manager and waiting staff.

'I'm not going to starve!' she shouted, clutching the carcass tightly as they tried to rip it from her grasp. Eventually, the woman let go and fell to the ground, where they left her, covered in dirt. Or perhaps I could try and recite poetry to passers-by like that writer who stood in the middle of a busy forecourt declaiming T.S. Eliot poems until people took pity on him and brought him something to eat.

I have longed to travel ever since I realised that the world's limits are not those of my city, Wad Madani; that the world expands so much further than the reach of my imagination. I used to love the idea of travelling without a specific destination, just setting off and roaming anywhere and everywhere. Like the little girl in the lounge, I thought of the world as mine for the taking, a precious sweet waiting to be unwrapped and devoured.

When I was a young girl, my eyes were drawn to the sky and I yearned to float up and see what lay behind it. What was hidden behind the clouds and the stars? Where did the sun go at the end of the day? Back then, there were times when the sky hummed with small planes, flying low over the fields. Whenever I heard a rumbling sound, I would run out into our back yard – jumping, screaming and waving my hands – convinced that the passengers would see me and wave back. I would run to every corner of the yard, shielding the sun from my eyes and chanting: 'Flying free, number three... Flying free, number three.' I didn't know then, and I still don't know now, what the connection was between flying and the number three. I'm not sure if I'd heard it from someone else – if it was a nursery rhyme or a song I'd heard about an aeroplane, or if I'd made it up myself – but it lodged in my mind, the beginning of an unfinished melody. On the ground, I fidgeted about, weightless with excitement, completely unaware that these planes weren't even carrying passengers, they were spraying insecticide.

I used to wish I'd been born in the form of a bird, awash with colour like a bird of paradise, those delicate and beautiful little things. I loved their sublime voices and the way the sun glinted off their brilliant blue feathers. They arrived at certain times of the year, visiting us at dawn and at dusk, lingering for a while in the neem tree in our front yard. I would sit on our doorstep for hours, listening to their joyful song as they flitted from one branch to another. They were a sweet blessing, and there was something so reassuring about their coming and going each year. I genuinely believed they came from paradise, and that the gap between their appearance and disappearance was the distance between the earth and the heavens. I dreamed of becoming a bird of paradise, resplendent with colourful feathers, a beautiful head, black eyes and powerful wings. I hid this wish deep down inside myself, seeking comfort in my imagination whenever I felt sad or lost.

The first time I let it surface was one evening, shortly after my mother passed away, when grief had started to creep into my heart. It was the evening after an autumn day trip spent in a nearby village with other children from my neighbourhood. It wasn't far, maybe forty-five minutes, but to an 11-year-old girl it had seemed like a great voyage. It was the first time I had left Wad Madani. I was struck by the lush green that carpeted the earth; fields of crops stretched out every which way around us, as we scampered here and there, free as wild cats. I inhaled deeply, savouring the fragrant air. The smell of the earth after the rain reminded me of my mother, relaxing and comforting me. Bursting forth like the dawn, this aroma felt like a fresh start.

I will never forget that day. We walked to the main canal that irrigated the fields and splashed about in the water chasing the birds. The other children ran and jumped through the grass, smearing themselves with mud and eating freshly picked tomatoes with the dirt still clinging to them. We were woozy with happiness, but this joy was to be short-lived. When I got home that evening, my brother Ahmad beat and cursed me for leaving the house without his permission. He hit me so hard that my entire body trembled with pain. Since then, a wound has grown within me, as great as the distance I longed to fly.

I dreamed of leaving Wad Madani to study at the University of Khartoum, like my cousin Ashwaq had done. She would visit and tell me hushed stories about Khartoum, making me realise that another life was possible. When I was accepted by the University, I felt my heart skip a beat. Finally, my prayers had been answered; I could leave home, move to Khartoum and get away from everything that had worn me down. I ran to my brother Ahmad's house, eager to tell someone the good news. I found him seated in the middle of the floor, playing with his baby son.

'You're not going to go gallivanting around in Khartoum or anywhere,' he said, without even turning his face to look at me. 'You're staying right here.'

Ahmad had always seen me as a blight on his otherwise perfect life. He forced me to stay in Wad Madani and to study at Gezira University. I made very slow progress, completing one class every two years. In my final year, my classmates and I were due to go on the annual field trip to Port Sudan; it was a trip that I'd looked forward to and dreaded in equal measure. When the day finally came, I was the only one in the entire year group who didn't get on the bus. As it pulled away, my classmates all waved at me from the windows and burst into excited chatter and song. I couldn't even raise my hand to wave. I stood there alone, staring at the tracks of the bus tyres on the ground. I was heart-broken; empty like a word without any letters. I decided never to go back to university again.

Now, here I am alone again, rusting away in an airport.

I'm suddenly aware that I'm cold and starving. I drag myself to the tap and lower my head to drink. I wash my face and stare at myself in the mirror. I look exhausted; I've lost weight and half of my hair has turned white. I think of Ashwaq, her youthful looks and jet-black hair, as if she's floated through life without a care in the world. She must have been waiting for my call for days now, and will no doubt be facing the storm of my disappearance.

I don't really know what happened to me that day. I remember being as happy as that little girl when I set foot in the airport lounge over a week ago. Only Ashwaq was there to see me off; she was the only one who knew about my travel plans. I'd thought that the moment I boarded the plane I would leave everything behind me and start my real life, the life I had dreamed of. Everything was arranged. I would have a seven-hour stopover, then get on another plane to another city, where Ashwaq's friend would be waiting for me.

Before my flight, I had wandered aimlessly around the airport, visiting the Duty Free and chatting with the staff. I smiled at everyone whose eyes caught mine, and when I went to the bathroom I shared half my money with the cleaning lady. Waiting was a pleasure. I didn't look at the clock once. I didn't feel time drag, nor did I sense it racing by. I savoured every moment like someone trying something new for the first time.

When the time came to board the plane, I stood in line like everyone else, dragging my heavy bags behind me. But when the other passengers started moving forwards, I found myself nailed to the spot. A mysterious force, some hidden obstacle, brought me to a standstill. The queue shuffled forwards, yet I remained perfectly still. More people moved forwards, but my feet refused to move. The people behind me urged me forward, but I couldn't put one foot in front of the other. They tut-tutted; I paid no notice. They raised their voices; I didn't care. The queue diverted around my solemn stationary form. A member of staff came and spoke to me, but I didn't hear what he said. He took me by the arm and moved me to the side, out of the way. I was blinded by fear. I felt a sharp pain in my stomach and a fever spreading through my limbs. My strength gave out and I fell to the ground. I didn't pass out, but I was oblivious to what was happening around me.

Everyone boarded the plane whilst I lay there, on the ground, alone and detached.

I look at my face in the mirror again. I have grown older, and somehow outgrown that desire I once felt.

The Beginner's Guide
to Smuggling

Zaher Omareen

Translated from the Arabic by
Perween Richards & Basma Ghalayini

IT'S 5:30AM. HOW I hate early mornings. Paris hasn't woken up yet; the streets are empty and depressing. The only people you see at this time are men and old women dragging their feet down the narrow pavements. Where is the Eiffel Tower? I stop and turn 360 degrees but I can't see it anywhere on the horizon. I can't possibly leave this city without seeing its most iconic landmark! It's OK, I'm sure Sweden has plenty to offer. The bitter taste of the sea lingers on my tongue. Why did *all* of that family insist on getting into the boat with us? Smuggling doesn't work for 'larger' people. Everybody should go on a mandatory diet before getting into those death boats.

The smell of the morning bread is mouth-watering, but distant. I'll be late if I follow my nose.

The cobblestone streets of Paris remind me of those of the Old Tawafra neighbourhood in Hama. There, all the narrow alleys where lovers meet are monitored by nosy neighbours, whilst here, no-one would flinch if they saw two people having sex in the street. What luxury they live in!

I keep walking and the sound of a muffled call to prayer walks with me, I can feel it echoing in my head.

'Gare du Nord. Gare du Nord...' I repeat the name of the station so I don't forget it. Where on Earth do they get these pronunciations from? It takes a hundred letters to spell a two syllable-word like 'Monsieur', what linguistic waste is this? While I was in prison, I was known to the other inmates as 'The Monsieur', I had no idea how it was spelt in French, and it ruined the nickname for me when I found out. But at the time, I preferred it to what the jailers called me: 'The Donkey's Doctor'.

As I wait at a red light, I look up at the balconies, carved with the precision of a clockmaker, balustrades gleaming as if they had just been painted.

A woman in her late seventies stands next to me. At least that's how old I think she is. I'm no expert when it comes to guessing distances and ages. She carries the weight of her body on a wooden cane that she seems to support as much as it supports her. She gives me an uneasy look. I smile at her. She doesn't smile back. The light turns green, we cross the quiet road together slowly. I can still hear the muffled call to prayer, intermittent, weak, out of tune.

Oh! It's coming from my phone! It's the morning call to prayer in Syria. 'It's better to pray than to sleep,' the Muezzin repeats.

'Never! Sleep is a thousand times better. At least!' I reply. How do you close this stupid app?

Back when I was in Greece, I had to trade in my smartphone for a cheap, temporary one to pay for a plane ticket to smuggle me this far. There were many Syrians in Greece, we all looked the same: broken and humiliated faces with no names. We were all individuals until we reached Europe, then we became 'Ferenja', as we say in Arabic. Abu Kalimera laughed as he said the word a thousand times a day, over pronouncing the 'J' in his thick Aleppo accent. He gave me his stupid phone and took mine as he handed me 300 US Dollars.

When in Rome, do as the Romans do. When in Greece, do as the Syrians do.

I dried my clothes on the sunny beaches of Kos, away from the prying eyes of the islanders, angry at the zombies emerging daily from the sea. I wouldn't have needed to dry them if it wasn't for that XL sized family, who got overly excited when they saw the land of dreams getting closer. The boat had tipped over with everyone in it. I'm a good swimmer, but a fool when it comes to everything else. I let my suitcase sink with all its contents as I started swimming frantically, fearing the coastguards who could send us back to Turkey if they caught us. All I had left was my expired Syrian passport from inside my underwear – I'd stashed it there.

'Kalimera, you son of a bitch, what happened to the passport?'

Abu Kalimera was in his forties or fifties. He forever had an unlit cigarette hanging from his lips, as if it had grown there in place of a Western accent. There were ten mobile phones in front of him, all ringing and falling silent in chorus. He handed me a blue passport with a bizarre logo on the cover. It looked like a cross between a crown and a mortar shell. 'Diplomatic Passport' was written across the front.

'Son of a bitch, you want me to be sent back home?'

'Take it easy. This passport belongs to the Hungarian ambassador to Turkey's husband. You're educated. Clever. Not like these sheep. Just memorise a few Hungarian words and you'll get through the airport. Go on, get yourself out of here.'

'And if it doesn't work?'

'Come back and I'll make you a new one; you won't have to pay a cent. I've added a Greek ID in there, free of charge.

Just don't try and use it to get out of Greece.'

'*A nevem Kaszuba Szabolcs, Koszonom. Dolgozom orvos, felesegem nagykovet, akarok utazni a hazamba.*'

God damn this language. The only thing I could memorise was my new name, Kaszuba Szabolcs. I have no idea what a 'Kaszuba' would even look like. It says on the passport that he's forty-five. I know I look older than my age but not by fifteen years! I call a friend already living in Sweden – that land of honey, cinnamon, and warm evening tea.

'What do Hungarians look like?'

'They look like all Europeans. Blond, white, tall, sort of muscular. Speak with a funny lisp.'

I stood in front of the mirror for two hours every day, pronouncing my new name. I tried putting the stress on the 'B' first, and then the 'Z', experimenting with different accents in case I was asked questions at the airport. I tried flexing to look more ripped, but it was useless.

In an Athens market as empty as an expired almond shell, I bought a 'Hungarian outfit' to make up for the lousiness of my new passport. A white shirt and a pair of jeans. Then I changed my mind about the jeans. An ambassador's husband wouldn't wear jeans! I bought a pair of dark grey trousers, and added a black briefcase like the ones security officials in Syria carry.

The day of the trip, I prayed two rak'as* for good luck and made my way to the airport. This was the only kind of relationship I'd had with God since I was a child: a strictly beneficial one. If I passed an exam, I gave a bit of money to the mosque. If I failed, they didn't get a penny. This time I decided to pay upfront.

It was a Sunday. The ticket to Paris was chosen carefully. Eight o'clock is what's known in the smuggler's code as 'the end of the end of the week.' I put myself in the ambassador's

---

*Units of prayer

husband's clothes and headed to the airport three hours early.

I didn't think I looked *that* Hungarian! My friends had always made fun of my fair hair. A 'foreign seed' they joked, referring to my grandmother's first marriage to a Turkish man, a remnant of the Ottoman occupation. Nobody forgets anything in that city.

My grandmother's Turkish husband got me through security and past the gates. But at the door of the damned airplane, a security guard stopped me, asking in broken English, *'Where are you from?'*

'Vagyok Magyarorszagrol... I'm from Hungary,' I replied in a terrible Hungarian accent.

He laughed heartily. The son of a bitch was on to me. He inspected my passport with painful slowness. A flock of pigeons flapped in my stomach.

Fuck you for this, Kalimera.

I hope he just sends me back to where I came from without detaining me for possession of a fake passport.

Where are those two rak'as I prayed? Now would be a good time for their effects to kick in.

'How many children?'

'Two'

He flipped the passport over again.

'Excellent job.'

He gave it back to me. No detention then! I took my empty suitcase and went back the same way I came.

'This way!' he shouted.

More pigeons flapped in my stomach. I did it. Those prayers weren't in vain after all! I was too afraid to thank him.

It was my first time on a plane. The air hostess guided me to my seat; she looked like the type of women I'd seen in films. Two British tourists sat next to me. They calmly buckled their seatbelts, I copied them, but I couldn't get the clip to work, so had to hold the belts together the entire trip.

The air hostess checked all the passengers; she smiled, which scared me. I'd heard that air hostesses were nothing but undercover agents, and that one look from them could get you thrown off the flight.

The scent of freshly baked baguettes fills the air in Paris. The call to prayer coming from my phone has finally stopped. I removed the battery completely. It was the only way.

The eighty-something woman disappeared into a house. Such strange balconies overlooking the street here, barely wide enough to stand on. How do they live like this! A car speeds past without splashing me as it goes through a puddle. I'm pleasantly surprised. The French are nice but miserable.

'How are you? I'm fine and you? Good, good. I'm a student, I'm a Doctor.'

I repeated this in my head over and over. Stepping off the plane, I prepared my fake Greek ID, and hid my Hungarian one. No one speaks Greek here; my terrible English will save me.

There were no security checks at Charles de Gaulle Airport for passengers travelling within Europe. A family friend helped me find a hostel in Paris; I forget the name of the place. I shared the room with seven other people and heard every possible sound a human body could produce. And don't get me started on the smell.

But it didn't matter. Sweden was one step closer! Even if I can still taste the sea salt. Next stop: Gare du Nord.

I had found someone who was driving to Copenhagen that morning through a carpooling website; the guy's English was as bad as mine, which was a relief! I booked my seat immediately for 80 Euros.

It will take 17 hours to get to Denmark, and then I'll take the train 7854 metres over the Öresund Bridge to Sweden. The train will stop at the border city of Malmo before heading to Gothenburg, the second biggest city, where about 550,000

Sami and Viking descendants live. There's also the headquarters of Volvo and IKEA, and the city's famous for its cinnamon buns, etc… I've read more about the history of Sweden these past weeks than I ever read about my own country.

Paris is so beautiful this morning. The quiet, grey streets are still wet from last night's rain.

'My name is Nicodemus Vasilios, I'm from Athena, and I'm going to Stockholm. I have scholarship in the university. Doctor. I'm doctor.'

I rehearsed this lie to perfection last night whilst staring at my Greek ID, just before I fell asleep.

I'd also prepared a list of topics to talk about en route. The first hour would be about the Greek culture, and how it differs from French culture. Second hour we'd cover ecology and botany. Third hour, toilet break. Fourth hour, nap time, as I'll no doubt be tired from the night before. Fifth hour, Greek food, and by then we should have reached our destination.

The car will head from Paris to Luxembourg, a country I'd never heard of before. Then it's Germany, Denmark and finally Sweden, where I will press the RESTART button.

The driver is called Daniel; I know nothing else about him, except his address, which is where we plan to meet. I arrive at 6:30am on the dot.

I try his mobile. No answer. Maybe he's still asleep.

I wait five minutes then call again, then wait again, call, then wait again. Nothing.

Fuck you, Kalimera.

'Go to France,' he said, 'it will be easier to get to Sweden from there.'

'But I want to go to Italy; that's a more guaranteed smuggling route!'

'Look, if France doesn't work, the next one is on me. How many times have you done this, now?'

'Five.'

'No worries! Sixth time's the charm!'

Oh Daniel… God of the roads and the roaring sea. Master of the city of lights, caster of long shadows. Man of dusty evenings and cold mornings. Answer, you son of a bitch!

All my prayers and invocations did nothing.

I sat by the side of the road and watched a van deliver papers to the kiosks. In Hama, we used to sell old newspapers by the kilo to the newspaper vendors. Five notes per kilo. Two kilos of newspapers – featuring the same photograph of our 'immortal leader' on the front each day – was enough to buy a box of Marlborough Red tobacco.

If I could get a cigarette right now, I'd have no doubt got myself out of this mess.

The phone rings.

Oh god of mobile phones, master of the luminous dawn, carrier of fertility to our barren lands, patron saint of the tired and hungry.

'Hello, yes, downstairs, near Gare du Nord, yes. No problem, take your time.'

I stand up quickly, brush down my Hungarian trousers and fix my Greek appearance.

I stand in military fashion in front of the address, pumped full of adrenaline. I feel like I can take out an entire Samurai squad with the blink of an eye.

The heavy Parisian door opens slowly, creaking a cheerful gothic tune to itself. As it opens it exposes a giant doberman with a frown on its light brown face. I shudder, squeezing my phone in my hand almost crushing it: an unresolved phobia since childhood.

The dog's appearance is followed a moment later by Daniel's – a tall, thin man in his late fifties. He is wearing a classic French coat, khaki-coloured. For a second, the two of them look like they're wearing matching outfits. Daniel waves blankly and walks towards me, the dog ambling lazily at his side. My heart thumps in my chest.

'You are Nicodema.'

'Yes, Nicodemus.'

'This is Winston.'

'Is he travelling with us?'

'Yes, he is super friendly.'

'Beautiful, very beautiful.'

I smile through gritted teeth, keeping a safe distance between myself and Winston. We head towards the car. Daniel opens the back door, and the dog, out of habit, jumps in behind the passenger seat.

All that stands between me and my new life in Sweden is a terrifying, slathering dog. What happened to those prayers you owe me, God?

'Fuck you, Kalimera, for such a trip.'

I sit down next to Daniel, and pretend to be calm, nonchalant. My heart leaps the first time Winston barks. I try to keep it together and ignore him, but it doesn't last.

Daniel isn't very talkative, which is for the best. He remains silent for most of the journey. He asks only two questions to which I give two answers; that seems to be enough. I stay perfectly still in my seat like a statue, frozen by the feeling of Winston's breath on the back of my neck.

Night falls and Winston starts barking. I remember prison. His barks are like the guards' voices during an interrogation session. No words. Only a series of rough, intermingled voices. No faces either. Detainees were always blindfolded. Dog-like sounds overlaid with intermittent screams of pain coming from all sides.

Winston's bark wakes me as the car comes to a stop. I open my sleep-heavy eyes. It's two in the morning. I must have slept for more than five hours! There is a police car by the side of the road. Four officers get out, one of them is a woman.

'Where we are?' I asked in my broken English.

'On the German-Danish border. Routine check.'

The pretty policewoman approaches my window, followed by another officer.

She smiles at me, I smile back.

'Documents, please.'

I reach for my wallet; I can't find my fake Greek ID. I must have left it under my pillow last night in the dorm. I look at the policewoman in defeat.

'I forgot my documents.'

I guess Denmark is as good a place as any to seek asylum. It's not quite Sweden – a bit smaller and not as cold – but I'm sure I'll get used to it. It's the world's number one exporter of fish, after all, and it borders Germany, Sweden and possibly Norway. Good standard of living, good education, easy language. I should have chosen it to begin with. It's better than Sweden on so many levels.

I calmly step out of the car as I'm instructed to.

Winston barks angrily.

I'm going to Denmark, you son of a bitch. Bark as much as you want.

Daniel silences him with a single look.

The policewoman takes my phone. She inspects it calmly; it's so old she can't actually operate it. She shines her torch in my face; I glimpse hers – so young, almost childlike.

'So you are Greek?'

'Yes, I am.'

'How you can confirm that?'

'I don't know. I'm sorry. I'm a student going to Stockholm to study program. I'm Doctor.'

As she makes her calls, I survey the darkness: a vast, empty landscape. Endless, open fields, ready to be used. I am shitting myself. I look around and choose a spot to run to. But the policewoman's childlike voice brings me back to the present.

'OK, how do you say good morning in Greek?'
'Kalimera.'
'That's right, you can go. Next time don't forget your ID.'
'Thank you. Thank you a lot.'

I walk back to the car. I stare at Winston triumphantly. You don't scare me anymore: you, or your weird blonde fringe.

I forget all my other names, everything, in fact, as I listen to my train crossing the Öresund Bridge into the darkness of the North Sea.

Phantom Limb

Fereshteh Molavi

On a Monday

WHETHER HE FIRST APPEARED on the screen or on the stage
makes no difference. Out of the blue he seized the spotlight.
His unseen Persian cat was meowing softly.

I'd woken up with an old idea that turned into a sudden
decision. I would start blogging again. I didn't know why I'd
stopped after arriving in Toronto. Perhaps there wasn't an
audience for it. Was there anything I could write online that I
couldn't already express in public? In Tehran, I knew why I
blogged. It was a crutch. A way for me to reach out to other
young people like me.

The phone broke my reverie. I could hear it ringing in the
hall. It was early, but none of my roommates would be home
– they had to be at the factory by 6am. I grudgingly picked up
the phone. It was Farhad's father. Long distance. I told him that
Farhad was at work and wouldn't be back until late evening.
He said it wouldn't be easy for him to call later. 'What can I
do for you?' I asked. Amid a sudden burst of Mandarin over
the line, I recognised his broken Farsi with a heavy Kurdish
accent, 'Let him know that his mother's right leg was cut off
last week.' I tried to dig a sound out of my larynx, but nothing
came. Farhad's cat appeared from behind his door and let out

a long, drawn-out meow.

We usually rehearse in the living room after dinner. I asked Najib and Varuzh to deliver the bad news to Farhad. After all, they'd both known him for the longest time. Varuzh and Farhad had met in Germany as refugees. Varuzh was Syrian-Armenian; Farhad was Iranian Kurd. Najib, who'd fled from the Taliban, had met Varuzh in Ankara before he too went to Germany. In their forties and in refugee status limbo, they work at the same miserable factory, making cabinets. I didn't know them when I first arrived in Toronto with a student visa and a dream of becoming a successful theatre director, free to write and direct what I wanted. I found these guys online, and soon realised that they would give anything to be on the stage.

When Varuzh and Najib came home, Farhad was not with them. He'd gone to see the owner of another factory in the hope of finding a job with fewer hours and better pay. We talked about how to tell Farhad the news, taking it in turns to play out his response. I wasn't much of an actor, so decided to give them direction instead. They didn't disagree. When Farhad got back, we immediately forgot everything we'd rehearsed.

On a Tuesday

I wanted to write a few lines about my own job; but neither it, nor writing about it interests me right now. What the hell can you say about a renovation company that hires people without work permits, and pays peanuts cash in hand? I was considering taking a job at the factory where the others worked, but it didn't sound like their boss was much better than mine. In truth, I was just curious to find out what they did all day. I wanted to go see it for myself.

I called my supervisor to let him know I wasn't coming in. I hadn't thought up an excuse, but could always rely on a variation of the cliché 'My grandmother passed away.' Instead,

I said, 'I just got horrible news from home – my mother's right leg was cut off.' I don't know why I did it. Maybe because the Persian cat was meowing softly next to me. As expected, my supervisor was deeply troubled by the news and suggested that I take two days off.

On my way to the cabinet-makers on Keele Street, I walked through Little Jamaica and tried to imagine how Farhad would feel passing through this neighbourhood everyday. Did he feel like he belonged? Did he feel safe surrounded by people who knew nothing of his home or language?

Their boss was a large man with an insatiable appetite. He interviewed me in his office while he ate breakfast. There wasn't that much he wanted to know. It wasn't the first time I'd looked for a survival job. This time I just pretended to be interested. He sat down in front of a burgeoning pile of food, lovingly prepared for him by his wife-cum-secretary. The first tray was piled high with bagels and cream cheese, coffee with milk and sugar; the second with some Iranian delicacies: two slices of toasted Barbari bread, Tabriz cheese, honey, cherry jam, butter, and a big glass of sweetened tea. As he ate, he spoke endlessly about his journey from lowly immigrant to top-class business man. His story didn't interest me. I'd heard it before: An Air Force officer for the Shah, trained in the US, worked briefly for the Islamic regime, fled to Canada, and started everything from scratch. My roommates distrusted him, suspicious of his political allegiances. But I didn't really care if he was an informant, or if he'd smuggled or trafficked. What amused me was his visible greed, brutally exploiting his jaws. Noticing that I was watching how he ate, he returned to complaining about his bottomless gut. I turned to look out over the workshop and imagined the hungry hours Farhad had spent, either in solitary confinement or during his escape over the mountains from Kurdistan to Turkey, without food or water. Thank God Farhad didn't suffer from his boss's greed.

After breakfast, I made my way home to study for the college admission test. Hardly had I started when the phone rang. It was Farhad's father again with an update on his wife's sufferings. The old man seemed to like these chats, particularly when the listener was a friend of Farhad, not Farhad himself. He was smart enough to realise that his son wasn't interested in talking to him. 'He never denies he doesn't get on with his father,' Varuzh once said. Yet Najib thought that it was more of a love-hate relationship. I held the receiver to my ear, occasionally responding with 'Oh, yeah' and 'Hmmm'. I was watching the cat walk from room to room, her tail in the air. Najib always says that such a graceful Persian shouldn't show her asshole. I averted my gaze and fixed my eyes on two pictures hanging on the wall beside each other. One was a small map of Iran covered with intricate painted patterns, much like a Persian cat's coat. The other was an old black-and-white photo in a plain black wooden frame, showing a young woman with lustrous eyes riding a horse, holding a gun in one hand and the bridle in the other. She had wavy long black hair over her shoulders and a wan smile on her lips. She was wearing a Kurdish man's puffed up trousers and turban. After hanging up, I stared at the pictures for a while through the half-opened door.

When Najib and Varuzh returned, Farhad was not with them. 'He had a sore foot,' Najib said. 'He went to get some painkillers from the drugstore,' added Varuzh. I asked about the picture of the woman on the wall. Najib said that she might be the girl Farhad had loved years before, but Varuzh disagreed. 'Oh, no, I think it's his mother. I know for sure he never saw that girl face-to-face. He only heard her singing in the cell next to his. How could he have a picture of her?' I wanted to ask Farhad about the woman in the photo, but Varuzh said that he wouldn't talk about it. When Farhad got home, I forgot to ask.

On a Wednesday

I woke up at 5am, and could hear Farhad moaning from the room next door. I tried to ignore it, but didn't last long. Sitting on the edge of his bed, Farhad was hunched over writhing in pain. I asked whether it was his right heel that was hurting. He nodded. When I tried to look at it, he snapped at me and said there was no bruise or cut. 'So, there's no reason to be worried,' I said gently. 'I'm not worried,' he snapped. He was in pain. He thought I didn't believe him, just like his old man never believed his mother. But after the surgery the old man called every so often to talk about his mother. Farhad shrugged. He used to call back home once or twice a month to speak with her, but after the operation neither she nor he bothered. If the old man could get through Farhad then he'd happily tell him all he did for her. To Farhad, his words implied that he hadn't done anything for his mother. I tried to change to the subject, asking if I should cover for him at work while he rested in bed.

Farhad's boss was not displeased to see me instead of Farhad. After all, Bottomless Gut needed young workers in good health with no work permits. At noon, he invited all three of us to have lunch with him in his office. Varuzh and Najib declined, preferring instead to eat their own sandwiches. Bottomless Gut insisted, waxing lyrical about the special dish his wife had prepared. He was very proud of his wife, particularly of her cooking. That afternoon, a new worker cut his hand badly. She gave him first aid, saving her husband from having to take him to a clinic and paying for medicine. Najib and Varuzh knew her talents also included convincing the safety inspector that the workshop followed regulations. But they both agreed her most remarkable skill was persuading workers, unhappy because of low pay or her husband's short temper, not to quit.

23

When we came back from work, Farhad wasn't home. The cat, reclining in her usual spot, ignored us. 'He must have gone for a walk,' said Varuzh. 'But his foot hurt a lot this morning,' I said. Varuzh reminded me that Farhad would take a walk whenever he felt stressed. 'Maybe he had another call from home,' Najib said. I remembered the latest call from Farhad's father, and that he spoke of his wife's panic at seeing a bulging stump instead of her leg. Varuzh, setting the table for dinner, said that it would be hard to imagine news worse than what he'd already got. Najib nodded. When Farhad finally came home, we began rehearsal and didn't speak of his mother again.

On a Thursday

This morning a loud crash woke me from my dreams. I jumped out of bed. The cane the boss's wife had given Farhad had fallen to the floor. The cat, who'd leapt over the edge of the bed, lowered her guilty tail. Bottomless Gut wasn't happy with a troublesome employee like Farhad, constantly complaining about a suspicious sore foot. Yet his wife had convinced him to let Farhad take a short unpaid break so he could go to the hospital for tests. I examined the cane to make sure it wasn't damaged. Farhad didn't move. It was a very old hand-crafted hickory cane with engraving on its handle. Bottomless Gut wouldn't appreciate his wife's generosity. I gently put the cane on the bed and got dressed to go with Farhad to the hospital.

At about noon, we left the hospital. Walking along the broad sidewalk of University Avenue in silence, Farhad looked a little disappointed that the tests were clear. What surprised me most was what Farhad had said to his doctor, that the pain had spread to the rest of his leg. When he described the tingling sensations, I wondered whether I should tell the doctor about the amputated right leg thousands of miles away.

When I came home without Farhad, the phone was ringing. I reluctantly picked it up. Farhad's father sounded agitated. He asked about Farhad, then spoke about the weather and the rate of inflation. I didn't mention Farhad's sore leg, convinced he wouldn't believe me. After a brief pause, he spoke of Farhad's mother. That morning, forgetting her missing leg, she'd tried to get out of the bed and fell face-down on the floor. 'Thank God, she only bruised her forehead slightly.'

When they got back, Najib and Varuzh listened to the news sympathetically. 'No wonder she's struggling to cope. She used to ride horses,' said Varuzh. 'Poor woman…' Najib muttered. 'She's only 60. She was barely 15 when she gave birth to Farhad. She married a man 20 years her senior and now the old man's still in good shape while she's declining rapidly.' Najib and I turned involuntarily and looked at the picture on the wall. Varuzh asked me where Farhad went after his appointment with his doctor. I shrugged. How could I explain to them what happened? We were walking on the sidewalk with our heads down, watching the women's legs as they strode by. A pair of shapely porcelain-white legs moved quickly ahead of us. I remember the clicking sound of Farhad's cane on the ground as we followed them. But when I raised my head, Farhad wasn't beside me. Varuzh didn't say anything. We trusted that he would make it back in time for rehearsal.

On a Friday

I opened my blog. Nothing. Only Farhad had bothered to read and share a post. Claiming that I had diarrhea, I left work in the early afternoon and rushed home to get the stage ready for our final rehearsal. Standing in the middle of the living room, I saw the cat sleeping quietly on Farhad's bed, her profile visible through the half-opened door. She was curled up beneath the map on the wall. My eyes drifted toward the picture in the black frame, the lustrous dark eyes beckoned me towards them.

I hung the two pictures in the living-room and dragged the mirror in from the hall. I was excited about surprising Varuzh and Najib. One boring Sunday afternoon, killing time on Bloor Street, my roommates and I ended up shopping for stuff that could be used for our future performances. It was Farhad who'd first been fascinated by this mirror laid among other trumperies on the back shelves of the Salvation Army thrift store. Najib and Varuzh were unhappy with the price. 'God knows how many things you could buy with 7 bucks!' said one of them. It was worth it, though. A bit rusty around the edges, the mirror was a middle-sized oval with a silvery-white wheat pattern at the bottom in a fine, thin silver frame – one of those you find on the mantelpiece of many houses as a wedding keepsake.

Varuzh and Najib returned home, but Farhad wasn't with them. They seemed tense, and didn't even notice my home improvements. Bottomless Gut had fired one of the labourers and ordered Farhad to unload one of the trucks. After twenty minutes, they'd heard a scream from the loading bay; a timber had slipped from Farhad's hand and struck his leg. Najib and Varuzh wanted to take him to the hospital right away, but Bottomless Gut's wife assured them that she could handle it. A couple of hours later Bottomless Gut came in, 'My wife called a minute ago. Thank God, it's not a fracture, just badly bruised. She'll take him home after he's done. Don't worry!'

I didn't dare ask if it was his right leg or left leg. In less than an hour, Farhad and Bottomless Gut's wife arrived at the flat. He was smiling from ear to ear, his right leg covered in white bandages. The woman was beside him, looking forlorn. For a moment I heard in my head a tune hummed by an unseen girl condemned to death.

On a Saturday

This morning I woke up in a good mood. Today was the day of our performance. Bottomless Gut called and asked us to work overtime, but we refused. I went out to shop, while Varuzh and Najib did some chores. Farhad, exempt from duties, was resting in bed, talking to his mother on the phone, playing with the cat, and listening to his favourite folk music. Ever since Farhad discovered that his right leg didn't work, he'd been in better spirits, more confident. He began to call his mother every week. The poor woman was shocked to learn of her son's misfortune, but it brought them closer together somehow. None of us could figure out how Farhad was feeling. It was hard to imagine him with only one leg, the other bent and tightly bound underneath the loose folds of Kurdish trousers.

In the afternoon we worked on getting the stage ready for our after-dinner play. Even the cat seemed excited. She was a free spirit, unable to be controlled. Before dinner we ran through everything for the last time. The set was minimal to say the least. There was a small candle on one side of the stage where Varuzh was going to play the role of Farhad's father, and an incandescent lamp on the other side where Najib was going to play Farhad. On Farhad's father's side we had the map on the wall and on the other side the picture of the woman hung. The small mirror in between reflected the father and son. The cat, meandering around the set, belonged to both sides. A second-hand tape player emitted the sound of a woman humming an old folk tune. Farhad said that it was similar to the girl he had heard in solitary confinement before her execution.

After our supper, Varuzh and Najib began. Farhad was sat beside me. We were at once audience and director.

On a Sunday

Whether Farhad disappeared on the screen or on the stage makes no difference. Out of the blue he seized the spotlight, then vanished. I was left alone with a silent cat, a creased map and a humming tune stuck inside my head.

I'd woken up with an old idea that turned into a sudden decision. I'd stop blogging in order to let my phantom roommates free me of my writer's block. I spent the morning running errands, studying and meeting with friends. At work, it was just me and Bottomless Gut. His wife didn't work weekends. I watched him eat and returned home without an appetite. I felt empty, and in a way betrayed. But who betrayed who? Was it time for me to leave? My roommates had once been with me and now weren't anymore. That was all. I went to my desk and turned on my laptop. A picture of the last scene stared back at me.

Farhad's in the middle. Najib and Varuzh flank him. All stand motionless, their expressions vacant. Each stand on one leg, with the other trouser leg folded up to knees with nothing below. Without crutches or canes, they somehow still look comfortable. Behind them is a white wall with a gloomy picture in a black frame. There is no sign of the mirror or any other props. Other than their pale faces, everything else, including their suits and shirts, is black. Their hands are hidden in their pockets. I can hear the sound of a woman's voice humming as I switch off the light.

Return Ticket

Najwa Binshatwan

Translated from the Arabic by Sawad Hussain

THIS STORY IS FOR you, my only grandson, who thankfully came into this world before I left it. I know I won't always be around to tell it to you myself, so I've written everything down for your sake. This is no bedtime story or lullaby; I write so that you can truly appreciate being born in such an open-minded village, where people, animals, plants, diseases and every type of wind pass through with great ease. No matter how much you try to hate Schrödinger, and our strange way of life here, be thankful that there are no walls or guards or laws standing in your way. Your parents weren't worried in the least about having you here, but rather what would happen to you if you were ever to leave.

Schrödinger is a cosmic anomaly; a place so unique it named itself. No matter how many names the villagers threw at it, it refused to go by anything other than Schrödinger. The name granted the village extraordinary powers; it could move through time and space, changing its orbit spontaneously as if it were the sun rising in one place and setting in another.

When you are old enough, I want you to appreciate this otherworldly blessing, and to respect the one thing that doesn't change in Schrödinger: the graves of the six American tourists that visited the village and never left it. Make sure to honour their souls on Remembrance Day, and make offerings at their

29

graveside, as is our way. It's said that Americans are born with ambition, while those born in Schrödinger are born satisfied. The American tourists were the first and last humans ever to visit our village; they stayed not out of love for the place, but because the walls of their own nation never stopped rising, day after day, until it was cut off from the world and the world cut off from it. Each attempt by an American tourist to scale the towering walls and return home proved fatal.

Schrödinger would hover over America twice a week, hoping to return the bodies of the six American tourists to their families. Yet, each time, the walls had been built higher and higher, until all that could be seen was the snuffed-out torch of the Statue of Liberty and her bird-shit-splattered crown. The American strategic intelligence experts eyed Schrödinger's movements with suspicion. They accused the village of acting with malicious intent, saying that feelings of inferiority – specifically geographical inferiority – plagued everyone living outside of their great nation's walls. But who in their right mind would want to live in a walled prison with people who can't even get along with themselves, let alone others? The American dream interpreters took a different approach, explaining Schrödinger's movements in relation to space-time theory.

The bodies of the tourists were an illusion between the folds of Schrödinger's soil. While the village was in orbit, the tourists would occasionally lift their heads to ask, 'Where are we? Are we there yet?' We'd tell them to hold on just a while longer, that not everything happens for their sakes and that there is a corresponding non-human existence in a limitless world that we can't control. Then we'd sprinkle fresh water on their graves and plant roses along the edges to protect them from the wind. All we wanted was for their souls to finally be at rest and for there to be peace between them and the people of Schrödinger.

We used to sit by their graves for hours, telling them stories about our daily comings and goings, certain that they understood us, despite the language barrier. When the eldest tourist woke up one day and asked if I'd managed to get a new passport, his brother raised his head from the soil, removed the plant stalks from his face, and said, 'No, not yet. She's still waiting for the references from the governor and the Committee of Textbook Dividing, which will never happen of course. Character references just to allow students to carry books on their backs!' He'd started to understand our strange ways.

At that, the elder tourist heaved a great sigh, 'What a load of shit. All this red tape and time wasting. They should just get on with repairing the potholes so that the students, bent over with their heavy books, can get to where they need to go.'

His brother closed his eyes and faced the sun, '*Why* is what escapes me…'

'Everything is intertwined,' I said. 'It sounds ridiculous, but it's much easier for me to get permission to travel to the moon than to visit another part of this planet!'

As the purslane vines continue to grow on the grave opposite him, the eldest tourist said, 'It's good that we died before America's prison warden came to power.'

★

Schrödinger's peculiar manner of travel has given us all life; a raison d'être. We never feel lost in our village, but rather lost outside of it. The village moves freely through space with us all still inside it, those above ground as well as below. It doesn't matter if you're Arab or foreign; there is no difference between us, except in good deeds and acts of piety.

We've travelled together far and wide. Once Schrödinger took us to Japan; one hour there felt like a glorious eternity, all

31

flashing lights, buttons and smiles. The hours we spent in Libya were also filled with laughter. It was a godless land, because the men there had become gods themselves, limitless in what they thought they could control. One man based his divinity entirely on the appearance of his paunch and kept women as a shepherd keeps ewes for reproduction. He made travel about gender rather than ability or need, judging each traveller on the underwear they wore rather than the passport they carried. Even the movement of planes in and out of the country was determined by men. If a man ordered a plane to be grounded, then it wouldn't take off. The passengers would get off the plane and return to their homes as if nothing had happened. Then another man would pull out his gun and order the plane to take off, so off it went to its destination without purpose or any passengers.

*

The only time I left Schrödinger alone was to visit your grandfather who had left the village a few months before to find work. I was pregnant with your father at the time, and was stopped immediately at airport security for travelling without a male guardian, a *mahram,* even though your father was inside my womb and he effectively *was* my *mahram,* according to those who strictly interpret the holy texts. The airport security still demanded that I travel with my husband or my son, not understanding that I was travelling with my son to see my husband. Their demands made no sense; they wanted my husband to come to the airport and vouch for me before I could be allowed to travel to him! Luckily, the guard was partial to a bribe, so I paid a hefty sum and he agreed to drop the fatwa against me for travelling without supervision.

Things weren't easier when I reached Triangle. There, I found an entire city of people that worshipped the number three. The triangle was a sacred shape and the people there adhered strictly to its angles. Everything came in threes; food, clothes, furniture, everything. The village was plotted on triangular lines, and entry was only granted to those whose dates of birth were divisible by three.

Fortunately, I passed the test at the airport and was granted entry into this angular world. My admittance was on the condition that I removed my striped headscarf and changed into something more 'triangular'. I was forced to remove my coat, glasses, watch, shoes, even my underwear before going through the detectors. The hardest part was hiding my shame from the guard; especially as the country had recently passed a law making it a crime to feel embarrassed.

After that, I reached an airport run by religious fundamentalists. All the guards spoke in holy verse and wore short trousers and unkempt beards. They prowled the airport looking for unaccompanied females, ready to lock them up or send them back to their husbands.

The customs officer asked me why I was travelling alone without a hijab, so I told him about the officials at the previous airport. He yelled that I was a *kafira*, an infidel, and that Allah would torture me in the eternal hellfire, burning me to a cinder.

I thought of your father in that moment, how could Allah burn me in eternal hellfire with a baby inside my belly; I could see no connection whatsoever between me showing my hair and the innocent baby growing inside me.

I begged the officer to have mercy on me, if only for your unborn father. He refused to lighten the punishment of hellfire, and declared that I should be forbidden from entering all seven levels of heaven. Apparently, he had a direct line to the angels above.

*

By the time I finally reached your grandfather, I was exhausted. The journey had almost finished me off. All I wanted was to bury myself into his chest. I threw my arms around him, but he was stone-like, unfeeling; it was like hugging a concrete column in an emergency ward in the hospital. I felt his hand move upwards and touch the top of my head. He was distant and cold.

'Where's your hijab?' he shrieked. 'Did you take it off?'.

It wasn't the reunion I had imagined. Instead of being happy to see me, your grandfather was furious, reeling off threats and insults, and rehashing every fight we'd ever had. It was almost as if he'd planned the whole thing the night before! I cursed him under my breath, repeating, 'Oh Allah, how did I ever love such an odious man. Oh Allah, intercede on my behalf.' But on he went; no stone was left unturned. I stood there dumfounded, waiting for him to bring up the time we fought over a TV show covering the election results of a country that shall remain nameless. I tried to calm him, asking him for forgiveness in my most pleading voice. He fell silent. I felt as if your father was in my belly, looking up at me, gobsmacked, demanding that I find him a new father, anyone but this sharp-tongued and unfeeling, bitter man. He kept repeating these words over and over, and then plucked from himself the only resemblance he held to his father; the hair on this head.

They broke my husband's trust in me when they removed the scarf from my head, and they plucked out my son's hair forever in that same moment.

They never think about the outcome of their actions or understand how they affect us. But I suppose the real disaster would be if they did know and truly understood, and still did nothing to change.

And so, this was how the first family get-together started and ended all within the walls of the airport. To make matters even worse, when your grandfather discovered that I wasn't wearing any underwear, he flew into another rage, divorcing me on the spot. This time, I really did hug the closest cement column I could find. I hugged it and cried, refusing to let go, as the planes took off, and landed in the distance, days merged into weeks, months into years. That airport became my home, never once did I cross the threshold. Instead, I became a woman without a past or a future, standing by the gates, going from airport to airport, without underwear, carrying an unborn child that pulled out its hair in protest.

I slept on the chairs in the waiting area a thousand times, selling tissues to travellers until I could buy a return ticket to Schrödinger.

My dear grandson, you will only truly understand the value of Schrödinger when the airports of the world search your heart, your pockets, the very pores of your skin, and leave you to waste away in their never-ending queues. Thankfully, our village is still a place where one can live and die as was intended; where light reflects and clean air reaches. If you are the wind, a bird, or even a stranger there, you're in luck, because you're still free, like those who are yet to be born.

Jujube

Ubah Cristina Ali Farah

Translated from the Italian by
Hope Campbell Gustafson

WHEN I THINK ABOUT Mama before the war, I see her sitting on her heels in the courtyard, hair wrapped in a green net, her face yellow with turmeric and butter, the precious ingredients of her beauty mask. She's vigorously stoking the fire, fan clutched in her hand, while her head nods almost imperceptibly, right and left, up and down, like the feathery flower heads that sprout from acacia in bloom.

The brazier is a cone of clay secured between her thighs. It emits ash and lapilli, and only settles when the embers are glowing hot, ready for cooking. Then Mama puts the water on to boil, though she doesn't prepare tea for us as other women do. Instead, she makes a decoction of roots to protect us from typhus and cholera, pneumonia and measles, because there are too many diseases in this world and you can never be too cautious.

Mama is a medicine woman by vocation, which is why the villagers both fear and admire her. My little sister and I wear bracelets of myrrh around our wrists, antidotes against snakes and sorcery. Mama's features, beneath the subtle mandarin-coloured sheen, are like those of an Egyptian goddess, engaged with secrets which weren't inherited, because it seems there were no herbalists among our ancestors.

She watches me and smiles graciously while I draw us some water. There isn't much left; later today I'll walk to the well and ask the cart-driver if he'll come fill the water tank. A barrel never lasts more than a week, and transporting it requires the strength of a donkey.

Mama built our house with flamboyant tree branches and braids of palms, mixing a paste of resin, dung and red sand to protect us from water and from the monsoons. At dawn, the walls are streaked with coral iridescence like in a sea cave.

I clean my teeth with a stick of *caday*, then gently wake my little sister who turns over on our straw mattress and hugs me, half asleep: she's still young, her curls are damp on the nape of her neck.

Each morning, we rise early and eat a breakfast of milk and sorghum before getting ready for school, carefully pulling on our threadbare uniforms and worn-out sandals. No one would comment upon our beauty if it weren't for our hair. Mama extracts gelatine from the leaves of the Jujube tree – the only soap or shampoo we're allowed to use – then sprinkles us with frangipani water and braids multicoloured ribbons into our hair. The wind transforms it into long vines filled with flowers. And thanks to her treatments, our hair has grown in extraordinary ways, black and lustrous like ebony, the fibres as ductile and strong as gold.

In the evenings, we take turns brushing each other's hair, crouched down in the threshold, coating our hair with coconut oil and separating it into sections that we twist like little tornadoes.

Recently, Mama managed to set up a small kiosk next to our house where people in the area can buy rice, flour, molasses and sesame oil; tomato paste, Omo detergent and fuel; matches, tea leaves and, remarkably, even henna dust. But people mainly stop by to ask about Mama's healing power and remedies, for which she never accepts monetary compensation.

She says it would be the same as making a pact with the devil, getting rich from others' misfortune. Her patients still insist on repaying her somehow, so instead they load her up with kilos of sugar, jars of tomato paste and bottles of oil.

Mama prescribes earth-almond flour, melted butter and honey for newlyweds; *qurac* pods for parasites; aloe extract for swelling; *carmo* leaves for broken bones. She also prepares a dessert containing acacia resin and goat milk for the holidays. Yet the most sacred tree for her, the one she always takes us to see, in the middle of her temple of medicinal plants, is the *Gob*, the Jujube. 'You see this stick,' she says, 'its roots grow in the sky, it cures ulcers and wounds, nausea and abscesses. Whoever dies with jujube seeds in their body goes directly to heaven.' From its flowers, she extracts an infusion for the eyes, and when it's the season, we go with big baskets to gather its fruits. When we get home, Mama candies them, dries them out and grinds them up so as to always have a reserve for her remedies and cures in the pantry. She sifts through the fruit with her mortar, a necklace of amber yolks around her neck, trusting in the miracle of plants.

Ah, but Mama doesn't foresee the war around the corner, the fleeing people who seek refuge in our village. The city burns and glows like a brazier, a filthy firework under the full moon. My little sister gets sick with an illness as horrible as the plague and Mama is no longer able to procure her roots, barks, berries. It's too dangerous to venture out there in the brush. The little one squirms on the wicker mat, being eaten by the fevers, the worms, the sores, her mouth filled with foam. Her beautiful hair falls out in clumps, leaving a mosaic of tiny scabs.

Defeated, Mama calls the cart-driver to carry her child to the hospital and entrusts me to the neighbours' benevolence, promising to return in a few hours.

Ayan Nur, a minor; country of origin: Somalia. Declares that mother and younger sister reside in the United States and requests that the procedure of family reunification be commenced. [Interpreter's note]

The world seems encased in ice this morning. I walk with my gaze lowered, like an acrobat on the frozen path. I see only the frayed corners of my duffle coat and the fringe of my scarf wrapped tightly around my shoulders. I'm not used to this cold. I can no longer feel my feet; I must have holes in my shoes. The sky is bent down towards the ground, carrying white clouds heavy with water. I try to feel my way forward, but my hands can't get a grasp on the fog. It's still early, I keep waking up at dawn. I pace back and forth, the light the colour of iron. Only in the war did I see such barren landscapes of sad browns and bronzes. The trees have a funereal look. I jam my hands deep inside my pockets and jog on the spot. The fog lifts slightly, and the hour of my appointment finally arrives.

I stop in front of the villa's wrought-iron fencing and hold my breath. The villa hides itself almost shamefully behind a veil of organza. The entire building would seem deserted were it not for a flicker of light in the second-floor window, so faint it almost looks like the reflection of the sky, if only the sky weren't covered by a blanket of clouds today. I push open the gate and step onto a path of dead leaves, some the colour of honey, others like embers and earth. Tall trees with leafy tops and tangled webs of thorns surround me. A gust of wind loaded with hail hits me like a handful of uncooked rice. The gate shuts behind me with a mournful sound, isolating me from the outside world. I am enclosed within an autumnal garden. I approach a heavy lead-grey door with large off-white stains. There isn't a bell but a cast iron door-knocker in the shape of a sphinx. I feel a deep anguish, but I need to be brave, the classified ad in the paper seemed promising.

As I cross the threshold, five crystal chandeliers light up and the door at my back closes silently, just as it had opened. I stand motionless in the centre of a constellation of vases filled with chrysanthemums, waiting for somebody to reveal themselves. There seems not to be another living soul in the villa. I'd almost resolved to leave when a black dog with a silver collar walks up to me. The owners of the house must be rich and eccentric. I'm petrified, there's nothing I can do about my fear of dogs, in my country we had to defend ourselves against the strays. He wags his tail, licks my wet shoes, his eyes the colour of bananas, his ears dangling. He seems to want to tell me something. I swallow my fear and decide to follow him into a small room with grey walls and a small already-set table in the centre. He sits on his hind legs, as though inviting me to take a seat. There's a cup of coffee waiting for me, a basket of pomegranates and – on a platter covered with an enormous silver cloche – freshly baked bread with butter and orange marmalade. I hadn't eaten anything since morning. Before I finish breakfast, the dog disappears. I tiptoe through a labyrinth of vaulted rooms, each one smaller than the last like a set of Chinese boxes. I can hear the faint voice of a child behind a half-open door. Could this be the one mentioned in the ad? I step into the dark room, immediately stunned by a miasma of sour milk. A nauseating stench, sharp like shards of glass. The voice, however, grows stronger, crystalline. My pupils get used to the dark and I clearly distinguish two little phosphorescent eyes, green like apples, green like sea fruits. I find my way in the dark, feeling the walls, in search of a light source. Here, a heavy curtain. I pull it aside slightly, afraid that the child might be bothered by the sudden brightness. Now I can see her entirely; she's standing at the edge of the crib, bouncing. In one of her hands she has an empty baby bottle, her onesie soaked with regurgitation and urine. And yet the child isn't crying, she's holding out her little arms towards me, almost chirping. She must be a little over a year old. I pick her up, automatically setting her on my hip just as I used to with my little sister. I'm no longer afraid, I venture down the hallway in search of a bathroom. The girl absolutely must be changed; the smell is disgusting. I enter a large room with a tub in the middle, set on feline claw feet. The faucet is made of brass. I turn it on to check the water temperature and I free the child from her wet onesie and heavy diaper. She'd worn it for too many hours, it was soaked with a yellowish stain. I wash her gently, I'm afraid of hurting her, she has pink spots all over her stomach and blonde hair like fine silk. Mama would be proud if she saw me now: if I find a good job soon I'll be able to join her in the United States, her and my little sister. I get a towel to wrap the child in and, upon leaving the bathroom, see the Signora for the first time. She's wearing an amaranth red silk slip, her shoulders covered by a scattered mass of fire-red hair. I back away, startled. She seems to be made of milk and freckles, two agate gems dangle from her ears. I've never seen so much exposed white skin.

'So, you've already met?' she asks enigmatically, her gaze impassive. I stammer, unsteady, the child tightens her grip on my shoulders, her little snow-white hands on my black skin.

Investigations conducted thus far are not sufficient to track down any direct relative of the client either in Europe or in the US. [Interpreter's note]

I watch as the cart carrying Mama and my little sister disappears behind the dunes. Mama turns her head back every few minutes, waving frantically until she is out of sight. The horizon is bathed in blood red; black lines sharp as knives radiate from the last slice of sun. It gets dark quickly, the neighbour looks out from the doorway and invites me to join her, but I tell her I can't leave, I have to watch over the house while Mama is away. She brings me a small plate of meat stew with a bit of rice. I eat alone, outside on the wicker mat, waiting for them to return. To calm my nerves, I grab one of the few jujubes left, they have a musky scent. I hold the pit in my mouth, roll it around with my tongue and then swallow it whole.

The lanterns agitate the shadows of passers-by and I hear quiet voices through the thin walls made of branches and dung. I pick up the hand-shaped comb and undo my braids, my hair is so long it almost touches the ground. The sky fills with white stars and I can see the Southern Cross next to the figure of a camel. Mama often tells us the story of a time when there was a terrible famine in a village in the North and the men decided to kill the camel of the sky and feed on its meat. So, they climbed a tall mountain and, as they still couldn't reach it, got on one another's shoulders until they were able to cut off its tail. In pain, the camel fled towards the South and then sat itself down, exactly as I see it now, ashamed of its lacking backside. Its large body comforts me, keeps me company. The camel saved itself from the greediness and cruelty of men and left a luminous wake in its flight, that of the Milky Way.

It's night when I'm wakened by a metallic noise like that of frenzied cicadas. I look through the cracks in the wall and quickly recoil: nearby houses are on fire. I rush outside and see women ruffled like wild birds, I see adult men falling like ripe fruit, I see the neighbourhood stormed by men meaner than stray dogs, abnormal creatures, with agate-like eyes blacker than the bottom of hell. The air is saturated with sulphur and dirty water; I move past the flames as lightly as a yellow butterfly.

A pack of ferocious dogs is at my heels, my already worn-out clothes have been reduced to rags. Thin streaks of blood line my legs. I arrive at the burial ground of my mother's temple. The jujube's burnt trunk is still smoking. I hug it, although certain it won't be enough to hide me. And suddenly I see a florescent wake envelope me completely. My hair takes the form of the jujube's spiky branches, it grows abundantly, hanging down towards the ground until covering me completely. My hair sprouts jagged and luminescent leaves and little white flowers in the shape of stars. The dogs howl around the base of the jujube, but they can no longer see me.

Numerous are the omissions and incongruences of the events described in the course of the hearing for a request for asylum. The client exhibits signs of torture and abuse. [Interpreter's note]

It's spring. The child and I follow the Signora through the garden encircling the villa. She removes dead leaves with a rake and piles them up on the side. She carefully clears the area at the foot of the willow tree. I tell her that the branches of the tree hang down like those of the jujube and I almost feel tempted to tell her about my metamorphosis. She nods sympathetically: I don't know the jujube tree, she replies, but you are quite right about the willow, that's why here we say it's weeping. Her face is motionless in the shade of a wide-brimmed hat. The child toddles unsteadily, attaching herself to my skirt; with her little hands, she picks dry hydrangea flowers, sits down in the grass and reduces them to dust. We help the Signora plant hyacinth bulbs around the cypresses. Clusters of wisteria with its intense aroma dangle from the fence. The Signora sings with an almost deranged joy about the first blooms. The child has her same milk-white skin tone; I protect her with a thick layer of sunscreen and follow her with a little umbrella: by now her curls go far past her shoulders. The Signora knows of my passion for hair, and yet she doesn't understand why I comb it with such care, why I coat it with regenerative creams, why I protect it from the wind and sun. The Signora's hair blazes like a flow of lava. She walks, dirtying her clothes with the rich soil and the orange pollen from the lilies. I wonder if her garden has a corner for medicinal plants too, and she responds coldly that she has no real reason to garden, no purpose other than beauty.

When it's time for a snack we go back inside, the child and I play with wooden blocks on a sand-coloured Persian rug. The Signora brings a silver platter, two cups of jasmine tea and a box of butter cookies. I take a container of fruit yoghurt out of the fridge for the child. While I feed her, she sticks her longest locks into her mouth, getting them all sticky. The Signora sips her tea and invites me to sip mine as well. Then, calmly, very calmly, she announces that soon she and the child will be leaving on a long trip to the United States that she can no longer delay. She knows that I dream of joining my mother and my little sister there, but, despite all her attempts, it's impossible for her to bring me with them; the laws don't allow it. But I can stay in her house if I like: the time will fly, it'll feel as though only a few minutes have passed by the time they're back.

Then she goes to the child, gathers her hair in her hands and adds, in her icy voice, that she'll have to cut it before leaving, because she won't know how to brush it in my absence. I stay silent, I leave my tea untouched. The Signora retires to her quarters. I decide I won't allow her to leave with the child, I won't allow her to cut her hair either. I'll wait for the Signora to fall asleep and escape out the gate with the child in my arms. I don't want them to disappear behind the hills, just like my Mama and little sister behind the dunes; I don't want to lose them to America too.

There is a reasonable amount of evidence to conclude that the mother and sister of the client had lost their lives during the massacre in the village of origin. [Interpreter's note]

Storyteller

Anoud

'IN 1991, I EXPERIENCED my very first air raid,' Jamela said in between gulps of rice and curry. She wiped the side of her mouth with her dirty sleeve, once white, now the colour of soot. 'It rumbled in my guts. I was certain we wouldn't live to see daylight.' The two men behind the counter of an Indian take-away in east London let her prattle away while she ate at a single corner table they'd set for her.

*

My parents had been preparing for it. They stuck crosses of duct tape on the windows and piled sandbags outside, covering the lower half of the windows. They figured that the pantry was structurally the safest place in the house if the roof collapsed, so they cleared everything out and converted the metal shelves on the walls into bunk beds for us to use when the bombs hit.

My sister and I were super excited about our new play room. We spent almost all of our time in there that week, doing our homework, playing Uno and gossiping about what the adults might be doing and saying.

'I want a pink gas mask,' I told my sister.

'When I die, I want my coffin to look like a race car,' she replied. We thought war was some kind of game, like the

47

Arabic-dubbed G.I. Joe cartoon on TV, and we were excited for it to start.

But when the first night of bombing began, I was petrified, crying hysterically and shaking so violently I had to clench my fists to regain some control of my fingers. I could hear the sound of bombs outside slicing through the air with a piercing 'voom'. It felt like I was about to fall off a cliff. 'Mommy!' I screamed with every blast. My mother reached up from the floor where she and my father were laying, and tapped the back of my hand to calm me down. My sister was curled up in a ball not making a squeak. Immediately after each 'voom' came a 'boboom' that sucked me deep into the mattress; then came the 'tatatat' of anti-aircraft guns. That loosened me up a little.

In between the vooms, bobooms and tatatas came the voice of George Bush over the radio transistor which my parents were glued to: 'We care about the Iraqi people and we pray for their safety.'

*

In 1996, I felt hunger for the first time in my life. The economic sanctions were hard.

'Mom, I want more eggs,' I asked one day. 'Have some bread instead,' she replied.

'But why can't I have more eggs?'

My mother stormed from the room, 'All I do is cook and clean in this house and no-one appreciates it! If you can't make yourself useful, then get out of my kitchen.'

I sat down and chewed quietly on half a flat bread, keeping an eye on my baby brother in his highchair, squeezing a piece of orange to mush with his stubby little fingers.

My mother turned her attention to a giant pot of mashed orange peel mixed with pungent chemicals. She was trying to make liquid soap for the dishes because there had been none in the local market in Baghdad since 1993. Along with all other imported goods, it was effectively banned. My brother started to cry so I pulled him out of his highchair and sat him down on my lap. He picked up a wooden spoon and banged on the table with it, while I stared at the rotating movement of my mother's wrist over the pot.

Suddenly, a tin bowl flew through the air at us. I screamed and we both fell backwards along with the chair. My brother had grabbed the tin bowl full of cooking ghee and accidentally tipped it over. The ghee was now in a puddle on the kitchen floor. I was on my back and my baby brother was trapped under the back of the chair. And where did my mother's priorities lie first? With the cooking ghee, of course! She quickly poured flour on the ghee to keep it from spreading. She then pummelled the dough with a snap of her wrists, completely ignoring my baby brother who was now panicked and crying.

Mother turned to me, 'What are you looking at? Pick up your brother!' We had floor food for dinner that night.

★

In 2003, I took shelter in my first bunker. My father decided that the safest place during an air raid was not the pantry after all, but a two-metre deep tunnel in the back garden. My mother resented my father passionately for ruining her flower beds. My parents fought with each other constantly. My brother and father laboured away with shovels for two weeks, digging an L shaped tunnel which they padded with thick rubber sheets to keep the damp out. We were miserable in that bunker. The grooved tin sheets layered on top didn't keep the rain from trickling in. The bunker was damp and cold, and the smell clung to the back of your throat. During the second air raid, my brother let out a giant fart. 'You're disgusting!' my mother, sister and I yelled as we climbed out of the bunker, in the midst of an air raid, to go back inside where it was dry, clean and warm. My father and brother gave in shortly after. We waited out the bombing with tea and sweets, watching a dubbed Brazilian soap opera.

★

In 2005, my best friend Farah was killed. She was a television reporter. I found out about her death at work when I was reading the daily news clippings that were circulated every morning to all staff. I didn't believe it at first, so frantically searched online for news. Images of her appeared on my screen. She was laying in an open coffin carried over the heads of tens of men, dry blood smeared on her cheeks and eyes closed. There were other images of her face down on the side of a road with a stain of blood in the centre of her back.

Some websites wrote that Farah's death was a conspiracy to kill all the elite Sunni Muslims. Others dubbed her a Shia martyr. Farah's mother was Shia, her father Sunni. I rushed to the bathroom with my head lowered, tears burning behind my eyes. People said good morning to me, but I ignored them. I locked myself in a cubicle for half an hour and cried. I splashed cold water on my face, and reapplied my make-up before sitting back down at my desk to catch up with my to-do list.

★

In 2006, I lost my cousin. I had never seen my auntie so sad; she looked like a burnt and half-melted lump of clay. She was sitting cross-legged on the floor, hunched over her lap, wrapped in swaths of black fabric. My cousin, her son, Anwar got 16 bullets to the chest and died earlier that morning. He'd called me just two days before to offer me a job with the news bureau he worked for. His wife yelled in the background as he made the offer. 'Don't listen to him. He's stupid. Make him quit his job.' Her voice got louder. I could hear them tussle for the phone.

'I'm serious,' he said. 'Think about it. It's much better pay.' The last I heard before he hung up was him and his wife laughing as she tried to grab the phone from him.

When I visited the family house, the living room, where the mourners had gathered was too much for me, so I hid in the bedroom where Anwar's wife and children were.

'I hate him! I hate him! I hate him!' she said. 'This is all his fault. I told him to quit but he wouldn't listen.'

Her five-year-old son walked towards her with arms outstretched. He looked confused. She swung her arm at him and flung him towards the wall. Stunned and afraid, he let out a muffled cry. I quickly picked him up, held him close to my chest. The smell of him reminded me of Anwar. Recovering from the shock, he began to let out a stream of tears and snot on my shoulder. I carried him away from his mother and walked back to the living room. He reached out to his grandmother, but she didn't notice him or me or anyone else that day. The news bureau called a week later to offer me a job.

'Absolutely not,' said my father.

*

In 2007, I came face to face with a murderer. Farah's killer came to see me. He came to brag. I asked him if he had killed Anwar too. He told me that he'd never heard of him. He was a businessman with a bald head, round belly and a thick mustache. His suit looked expensive but he smelled of cheap cologne.

He said, 'We don't like Shia women walking into our mosques with film crews. So my cousins and I decided to put them in their place.'

I wanted to tell him she was half Sunni but I didn't think it mattered to him. He told me how he had hiked up her skirt and raped her. He confused me with his conflicting stories and I couldn't understand if he had murdered her himself or ordered others to. Farah's hair colour kept changing in his story from black to blonde to red. He spoke about how he enjoyed pulling her nails out and peeling the skin from her arms with his knife. I wanted to say, 'We buried Farah with her skin and nails intact,' but my tongue was tied. I caught myself faking a smile, quietly waiting for him to finish talking. I even shook his hand when he stood up to leave. That day was the first time I lost my appetite for food. It was also the first time I tried to masturbate and felt nothing.

★

In 2011, I had my first close encounter with a car bomb. I was with a colleague from work driving home when it went off. Our car flew up into the air and came crashing back down again, front tyres first. We reached out for one another, finding our way through the airbags. I was shaking from head to toe like during my first air raid.

We got out of the car to see the carnage – 10 or so cars ahead, dead bodies riddled with holes. They looked like old and torn up sandbags. Pools of blood were mixed with mud and covered by a thin surface of soot. It was extremely hot. Flies stormed in by the hundreds for the feast. My knees and shins felt like they were melting underneath me. I can't explain it. They felt like they were turning into liquid. He helped me back to the car. I was shaking, so was he. He squeezed me tightly, told me I was beautiful then kissed me hard. I bit his lower lip. He dug his nails into my sides. I felt my insides come back to life. That was not me on the side of the road, lifeless, covered in dust and riddled with holes like a torn-up sandbag. I lost my virginity in 2011.

★

In 2012, I came to London for a workshop paid for by my job. I raised my arms in the air and cried, 'Asylum, asylum' as soon as it was my turn to approach the immigration counter at Heathrow airport. Other passengers waiting in line looked alarmed. Airport security rolled their eyes at me then took me to a detention centre. They let me go after five or six months, I can't remember. I was left roaming the streets of London with £200 pending a court hearing ahead of my asylum request. I never spoke to my family again. They had no idea how to reach me. They ceased to exist.

In 2012 I discovered alcohol.

In 2013 I was granted asylum.

In 2013 I tried to kill myself and stopped with the fifth pill before I pushed my fingers down the back of my throat and vomited the rest out.

In 2013 my GP said I needed to drink less.

In 2014 I had sex with a stranger in a toilet stall. He was rough, and I was terrified.

Between 2012 and 2014, I started and lost many cash-in-hand jobs.

★

In 2014, I saw the remains of a Baghdad car bomb, a mangled heap of metal, mounted on a clean white podium under a blinding spotlight at the Imperial War Museum in London. I felt sorry for it for being so out of place and so nakedly on display. A crowd of people in shorts, summer dresses, funny t-shirts, baseball caps and purple braids gathered in a circle around the car. The slabs of dented metal were so mangled they looked like tens of human guts pressed together and left baking in Iraq's burning sun until they were bone-dry.

But what do these people know? Staring at it. Taking photos. The car bomb made me feel nostalgic and homesick. I tried to touch it. Security cornered me and threw me out. I decided to call my parents in Baghdad, but I'd forgotten their phone number.

In 2014, I discovered meth.

In 2014, I became angry.

In 2014, the nice family who helped with my asylum case threw me out on the street. I was sorry for hitting them and trying to steal their things. I didn't mean to. I was high. I tried apologising but they locked me out and threatened to call the police.

*

The two men behind the counter at the Indian takeaway were now starting to regret feeding the woman.

'Bro, she's not shut up since she got here,' one of them said.

The other man waved his hand, 'Let her be, bro.' Jamela, oblivious to her surroundings, was busy pressing her dirty fingers on the side of the foil plate to scavenge every last grain of rice.

Suddenly, she raised her eyebrows, stood tall. The glazed look in her eyes became sharp. The face of Donald Trump appeared on the television in the corner. 'Donald J. Trump is calling for a total and complete shutdown of Muslims entering the United States until our country's representatives can figure out what the hell is going on.'

'Fuck you!' Jamela yelled waving a fist at the television. The two restaurant workers looked alarmed; they were used to the timid Jamela. Yet, there she was standing and waving her fist at the television. 'Fuck you!' she yelled again. 'That was my car bomb. Mine! And they had no right not letting me touch it. Fucking tourists.'

'Bro, she's talking about a bomb! Call the police.' The man hid away in the kitchen to make the call while the other stood behind the counter nervously watching Jamela fling her fists in the air, cursing.

Two large police officers arrived. They dug their hands deep under her armpits and dragged her out of the takeaway, hands cuffed behind her back. She was thrown into the back of the police car.

'In 1991 I experienced my first air raid...'

'We're taking her to the station for questioning,' one of the officers said over the radio. 'She looks harmless, probably just a homeless crack head,'

Jamela made herself comfortable in the back seat. She and the officer made eye contact through the rear-view mirror. Jamela began again: 'In 1991, I experienced my first air raid...'

The Slow Man

Wajdi al-Ahdal

Translated from the Arabic by William M. Hutchins

The Year 100 According to the Babylonian Calendar

TWELVE CARAVANS ARRIVING FROM the north were stopped and denied entry to Egypt on reaching the checkpoint at Gaza.

No prejudice was behind the ban; truth be told, the Egyptian Commander of the border guards on the northern frontier – a man named Tanah Ramba – was simply one of the slowest men ever born.

Now, some might say that the Commander's lethargy was no one's business but his own. Yet, we live in an interconnected world and everything can change in the blink of an eye.

It took the Commander three hours on foot to reach the border post from his residence, even though it wasn't far and a brisk walker could have made the same journey in twelve minutes.

The Commander had an odd gait; after each step forward, he would stop, look ahead, and inhale deeply, taking in as much air as his lungs would hold. Seconds later he pounded the earth resolutely three times while glancing back at his lame left foot, which he then pulled forward with three jerks.

He had devised this technique himself, if only to discourage people from entering Egypt. And to rile them further, he spent as little time as possible at the border crossing.

He would return to his lodgings in a light carriage drawn by a thoroughbred horse.

People gossiped about the Commander behind his back, spreading a rumour that he was kin to the pharaoh and had royal blood flowing in his veins.

He was barely fifty, but his lean frame and grey hair made him look much older. Those who saw him, and didn't know any better, guessed he must be at least a hundred years old.

His ebony-black concubine, a woman of uncertain lineage, shaved his face each morning and moisturised his skin with oil scented with frankincense. Despite all her ministrations, his complexion had never regained its lustre; she could not contrive to make his face look splendid enough to match his rank.

A few years earlier, he had eaten a poisoned meal of kidneys in Beersheba. Although he had escaped death, his health never fully recovered. The poison had discoloured his face, turning his lower jaw coal-black and dotted with flame-red pimples. He also suffered from the occasional muscle spasm, making it almost impossible for him to move or sleep.

The Commander insisted that it was the Babylonians that had poisoned him, because who else would benefit from his demise.

Everyone dismissed these allegations, but the Commander would soon be proven right.

Only a month after this supposed attempt on the Commander's life, the pharaoh died – again through poison. An inquest was underway to identify the perpetrator or perpetrators.

The Commander was absolutely convinced that a network of Babylonian spies had assassinated the pharaoh with poison.

Acting on his own authority, without asking permission from the capital, which after all was in a state of mourning, the Commander issued a travel ban preventing Babylonians – and the people ruled by them – from entering Egypt.

He justified his ban as a temporary measure, designed to keep Egypt and its territories safe from the infiltration of enemies.

Around noon, the Commander was sitting on his special chair in front of the control post, warming himself in the sun's rays. Chill winds from the sea were blowing rotating, petal-like clouds towards them, harbingers of a quickly approaching winter storm. The Priest Barsis had been anxiously waiting for the Commander to appear, biting down hard on his lip.

The Commander held a hand over his coal-black chin and asked, 'What does the Lord's servant desire?'

The Priest dried the sweat from his brow and replied, 'Soldier of Amun, a momentous event!'

'I'm listening.'

'When we were praying this morning, the sacred bird – the Ibis – flew into the temple. I have served for thirty years as the custodian of the House of Amun in Gaza, but this is the first time such an auspicious event has occurred.'

'So does this mean I'll die?' the Commander quipped.

The Priest ignored this and continued very seriously: 'This is a sign from the Lord Amun. We must not ignore it.'

The Commander fidgeted. 'You know much more about such matters than I do.'

'I followed this messenger of the Lord when it left the temple and saw it land over there.' He pointed to the East with his finger and continued: 'On the hump of a camel belonging to the Ishmaelite caravan.'

'It may have thought they were rats!' the Commander laughed.

Sweat poured down the priest's forehead, but he tried to look calm.

'I implore you; send your troops with me to search that caravan.'

The Commander consented to the Priest's request and sent a squad of soldiers off with him.

*

Egyptian merchants came to Gaza in throngs, offering fire-sale prices for goods from the banned caravans. Some grudgingly sold the goods they had hoped to carry to Egypt, and others simply headed back to their home countries, refusing to sell at such prices.

One caravan remained because the men were struggling to reach a consensus. They were in no hurry to leave, but bargained so aggressively for fair prices that the Egyptian middlemen eventually abandoned them.

Later that day, the Commander's men approached the Ishmaelites and surrounded them as they ate. The Priest ordered the soldiers to search the caravan by decree of the Commander of the Egyptian border guards.

The Priest oversaw the search personally and the Ishmaelites brought him their sacks one-by-one for inspection. The Priest searched through the sacks but found nothing unusual in them: just the customary cargo of high quality incense, cinnamon, myrrh, frankincense, and other expensive fragrances that temples are eager to acquire and that the wealthy purchase at exorbitant prices.

The Priest continued to prowl around the caravan, refusing to leave until he'd found something, anything, that would give him answers. He wasn't sure what that something was, but could sense he was making the Ishmaelites nervous.

Then he asked to speak to the leader of the caravan. A distinguished shaykh with a beard like a lion's mane appeared, his eyes glittering and flashing.

The Priest stared at him for a moment and then addressed him in Akkadian with a Babylonian accent:

'Where are you from?'

'Mecca.'

'I've heard of it. Now that you've been denied entry to Egypt, what are you going to do?'

'We're going to camp here until you let us in.'

'You're obstinate,' said the Priest. 'Will you let me help you?'

'Can you?' asked the Shaykh.

'I can obtain an exemption from the travel ban for you from the Commander.'

'That's very kind of you. We'd give you a tenth of all the cargo on my camels in return.'

The Priest smiled. 'I'll do this free of charge.'

The Shaykh was baffled and sceptical.

The Priest pointed to a child lying sound asleep on his side, as bees buzzed gently around his head. 'Is the boy sick?'

'No, it's just that the trip exhausted him.'

'You all are so cold-hearted: a young boy like that can't stand the hardship of such an expedition.'

'We found him abandoned in the desert. The boy was famished and naked. So, we fed him, clothed him and brought him along with us.'

The Priest approached the sleeping child and began to scrutinise him. He felt the child's forehead. 'He has a fever. I'll send for some medicine.'

The master of the caravan remained silent. He was busy trying to decipher the Priest's intentions.

The Priest took a step back when it became clear that the bees did not want him near the child.

'Is he Canaanite?'

'No, he's Hebrew,' said the Shaykh.

'I thought I saw a bird land here earlier,' the Priest said.

'You're right. It was a bird with a black head and white wings. The tips of its feathers were black as if it had dipped them in ink. Is it a bird that brings good luck?'

The Priest tapped his bald head with a finger and said, 'I think so.'

★

Under cover of darkness an unknown man slipped into the Commander's fortress-like residence. Two people whispered together, joking. 'What's new?'

'The high Priest of Amun visited us tonight.'

'That devil Barsis! What did he have to say?'

'He asked my master to grant a special permit for the Ishmaelite caravan to enter Egypt.'

'Ha! Did your master agree?'

'Yes.'

A brief silence.

'What's on your mind?'

'I'm wondering what interest that devil Barsis has in that caravan.'

'I heard him mention a sign from the Lord Amun... and something about a boy who will be important.'

'So that must be it,' said the man jumping to his feet.

'What's gotten into you?'

'Come on! There's no time to lose.'

★

The Commander arrived as his men were beginning to eat lunch. He thought he would find the Priest waiting for him. When he didn't see him, he inquired only to be told that he had left that very morning to follow the Ishmaelite caravan. The Commander sighed, relieved that the caravan had finally given up hope of entering Egypt and had departed far away from the nation's borders.

His deputy informed him that the Ishmaelite caravan had left pursuant to his orders. The Commander was dumbfounded and said he had never issued any such order. He was truly shocked and allowed his ugly, discoloured jaw to dangle down when his deputy showed him the papyrus document stamped with his seal.

But because he was so tired, slow and indecisive, the Commander did nothing. He did not grasp the full scope of the conspiracy till he returned to his residence and found that his favourite concubine had vanished.

The next day he rejected his deputy's suggestion to send troops to bring back the Ishmaelite caravan. He was content to wait for the Priest to return.

He had no idea that the Priest's head had already rolled off his shoulders and that he was unlikely to return any time soon.

*

128 Babylonian Era

Once eighty percent of the Egyptian populace perished in the famine, the powerful Babylonian army was able to extend its reign to Egypt.

The Israelite tribe was eliminated in mysterious circumstances.

Babylonian engineers finally erased Egypt from the map by diverting the course of the Nile to flow south into Lake Chad rather than north to the Mediterranean.

1000 Babylonian Era

After centuries of massive engineering efforts that employed the manpower of millions of slaves, the waters of the Nile finally reached the Senegal River and flowed into the Atlantic Ocean.

The Babylonians continued settling peoples from Asia on the banks of this mighty river.

3900 Babylonian Era

People no longer knew anything of monotheist religions. Worship of the god Marduk prevailed, and his temples were scattered throughout the Earth's seven continents. (The Babylonians discovered a seventh lurking beneath the Indian Ocean and raised it, making it fit for human habitation.) Dakar was the world's spiritual capital.

The Festival of the New Year was celebrated each spring with the ritual copulation of the God Marduk to one of his priestesses.

Europe was by now completely abandoned, and history books no longer made any reference to the Greeks or Romans.

4000 Babylonian Era

When electronic chaos cracked the space-time cone of four-dimensional existence, previously unknown creatures slipped through this gap and claimed, on their arrival, to be the planet's primordial species who were returning to colonise it once more.

They referred to themselves as 'They Who Have Come to Retrieve the Earth from Mankind.'

4011 Babylonian Era

The end of the human race was accompanied by the hegemony of creatures far more intelligent and far more evil than people had ever been.

About the Authors

Wajdi al-Ahdal is a Yemeni novelist, short story writer, screenwriter and dramatist. He is the author of several collections of short stories and four novels, including *A Land Without Jasmine* (published in English by Garnet, 2012). His novel *Mountain Boats* was confiscated by the Yemeni Ministry of Culture for insulting 'morality, religion, and conventions of Yemeni society', and a campaign against the book drove him into exile for a number of years. He now lives in Saana.

Anoud is an Iraqi-born author living in Algiers. Her story 'Kahramana' was featured in *Iraq + 100* (Comma Press).

Najwa Binshatwan is a Libyan academic, novelist and playwright. She is the author of three collections of short stories and three novels, including *The Slaves' Pen* (shortlisted for IPAF 2017). In 2005, her novel *The Horses' Hair* won the inaugural Sudanese al-Begrawiya Festival prize, in the same year that Sudan was Capital of Arab Culture. She was chosen as one of the 39 best Arab authors under the age of 40 by the Beirut39 project and her story 'The Pool and the Piano' was included in the Beirut39 anthology.

Ubah Cristina Ali Farah was born in Verona, Italy, of a Somali father and an Italian mother. She grew up in Mogadishu but fled at the outbreak of the civil war at the age of eighteen. She is a poet, novelist, playwright, and oral performer. She taught Somali language and culture at Roma

Tre University and is currently based in Brussels. She has published stories and poems in several anthologies and in 2006 she won the Lingua Madre National Literary Prize. Her novel *Madre piccola* (2007) was awarded the prestigious Vittorini Prize and has been translated into Dutch and English.

Born in 1979, **Rania Mamoun** is a Sudanese author, journalist, and activist. She has published two novels in Arabic – *Green Flash* (2006) and *Son of the Sun* (2013) – as well as a short story collection *Thirteen Months of Sunrise,* which will be published in English by Comma Press in 2018. Her short stories have been published in various magazines and anthologies, including *The Book of Khartoum* (Comma Press, 2016), the first ever anthology of Sudanese short fiction in translation. She has also worked as culture page editor of *Al-Thaqafi* magazine, a columnist for *Ad-Adwaa* newspaper and presenter of the 'Silicon Valley' cultural programme on Sudanese TV.

Born in Tehran, **Fereshteh Molavi** is the author of several works of fiction, short stories and essays including *The House of Cloud and Wind*, *The Sun Fairy* and *The Departures of Seasons*, which was admired by the Mehregan Literary Award (Tehran, 2012). While in Iran, unable to publish some of her works due to censorship, she compiled a comprehensive bibliography of short stories in Persian and also translated numerous works by internationally-known writers. She moved to North America in 1998, and was previously a research librarian and the Persian bibliographer at Sterling Library, Yale University. She now lives in Toronto and divides her time among writing, organizing literature events, and advocating freedom of speech and human rights in Iran.

Zaher Omareen is a Syrian writer and researcher based in London. He has worked on independent cultural initiatives in Syria and Europe, and co-curated exhibitions on the art of the Syrian uprising. His short stories have appeared in Words Without Borders among others, and he recently co-edited and contributed to *Syria Speaks: Art and Culture from the Frontline* (Saqi Books, 2014). He is currently working on a collection of short stories drawn from the collective memories of the 1982 Hama massacre.

About the Translators

Ruth Ahmedzai Kemp is a British literary translator working from German, Russian and Arabic into English. She graduated from Oxford University in 2003 where she studied Russian and German, did an MA in Translation and Interpreting at Bath University, and then started studying Arabic intensively while already working as a professional translator. She has a Postgraduate Diploma in Translation in all three of her language combinations. Ruth has translated novels by Fadi Zaghmout, Hanna Winter, Kathrin Rohmann and Yulia Yakovleva, and non-fiction books on nature, history, politics, civil rights, child psychology, linguistics, art history and literary criticism. She has also translated plays from Russia, Syria and Lebanon, and several short stories and children's picture books.

Basma Ghalayini is an Arabic translator who has previously translated short fiction for Maaboret: The Short Story Project and Commonwealth Writers. She was born in Gaza, and grew up in the UK until the age of eight, before returning to the Strip.

Sawad Hussain is an Arabic translator and litterateur. She holds a MA in Modern Arabic Literature from the School of Oriental and African Studies and regularly critiques Arabic literature in translation. She was co-editor of the Arabic-English side of the award-winning Oxford Arabic Dictionary (2014), and has translated the work of Fadi Zaghmout, Sahar Khalifeh and Saud Al Sanousi among others.

William M. Hutchins is an American academic, author and translator of contemporary Arabic literature. He He is currently a professor in the Department of Philosophy and Religion at Appalachian State University in Boone, North Carolina. His translations include the Cairo Trilogy by Egyptian Nobel Prize-winner Naguib Mahfouz and A Land without Jasmine by Wadji al-Adhal. He has also translated the work of Tawfiq al-Hakim, Nawal El-Saadawi, Muhammad Khudayyir and Ibrahim al-Koni, and others.

Hope Campbell Gustafson graduated from Wesleyan University in 2012. She is an MFA candidate in the Literary Translation Workshop at the University of Iowa. Her translations have been published or are forthcoming in *Exchanges Literary Journal*, *Asymptote*, and *The Brooklyn Rail*.

Perween Richards is a literary translator from Arabic. She attended the Translate at City summer school in London in 2016, and was one of two winners of the school's annual translation competition, sponsored by Comma Press. She was recently awarded an English PEN Translates grant to translate *The Sea Cloak* by Nayrouz Qarmout, which will be published in English by Comma Press in 2018.